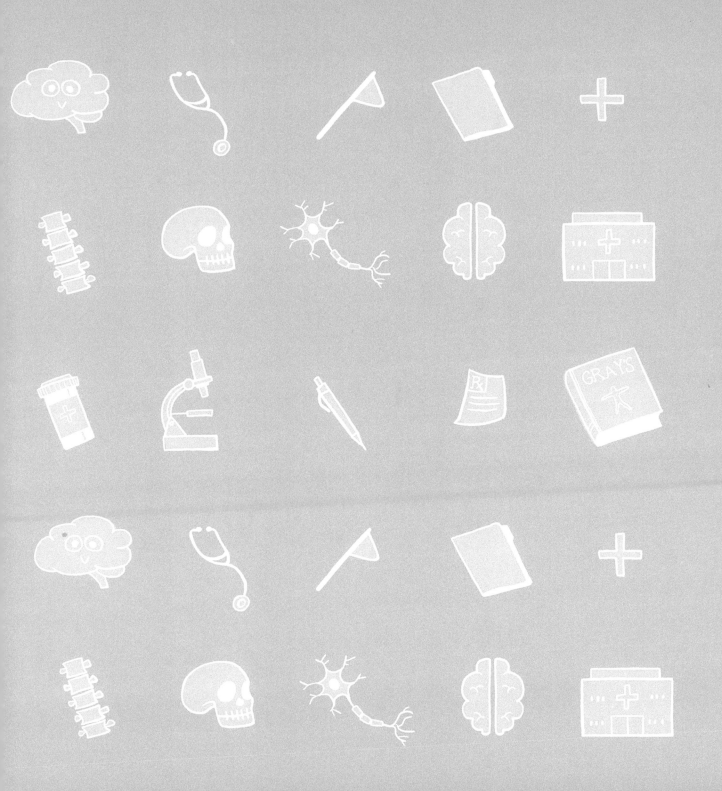

This Book Belongs to:

_____

_____

_____

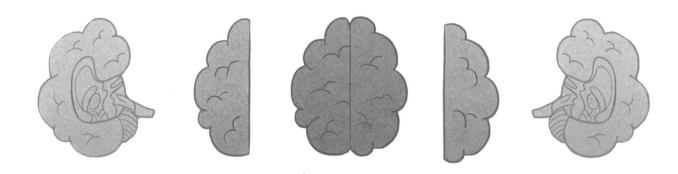

Published by Cabin Health Inc.
Text copyright (C) 2021 by Ali Zaman
Illustration copyright (C) 2021 Tanya Zaman

To our father, Taimur Zaman, a kind and compassionate neurologist.

Neurologists
are detectives
of the

BRAIN

They're on the hunt for
bandits & bozos up to no good.

Sometimes they cause headaches.

And sometimes they make you SHAKE

They might
make you
forget things

Or fall over when you walk

A long time ago, 3 doctors
discovered how the brain worked.

They did a big
show-and-tell for
doctors around the world.

And then, neurology was born.

Neurologists spend a
long time in school

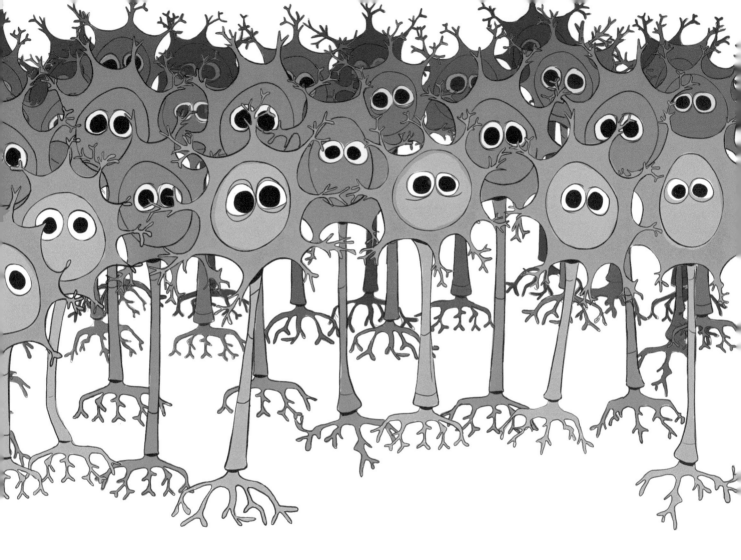

To learn what all **86 BILLION** neurons in the brain do.

After school, new neurologists
follow around old neurologists

To learn how to help any patient
that walks in the door.

First the neurologist asks the patient how they feel.

This is called taking history.

My left hand is shaking

I'm forgetting things

I fall over when I walk

Then the neurologist watches
the patient do funny activities.

This is called the
neurological exam.

Walk 5 steps

Lift your arms

Touch your nose

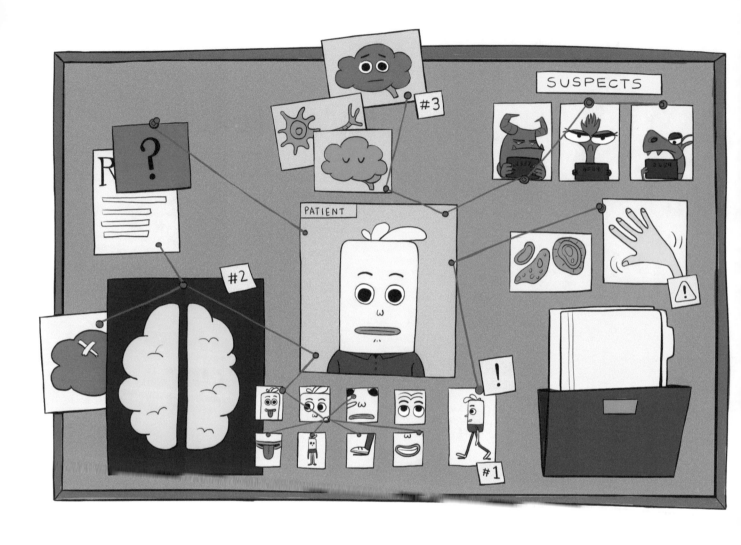

It's time to round up
all the clues...

And send the patient for testing.

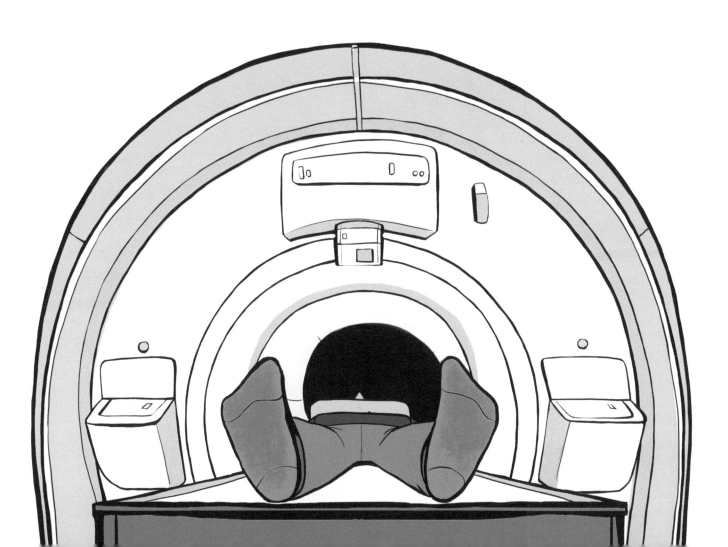

Testing lets neurologists look into your brain.

It's kinda like having X-ray vision.

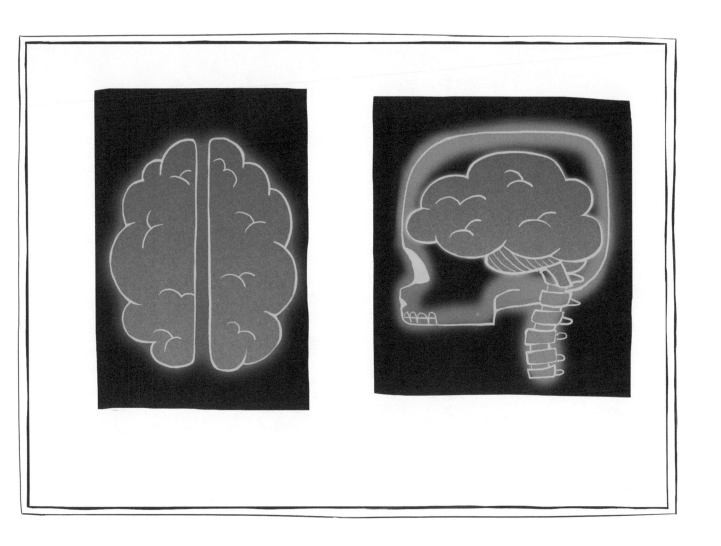

Now, it's finally time to tell
the patient what's going on.

"you have shaky arm syndrome."

"Here's some medicine to make the shaking go away."

After the *patient leaves,*
neurologists write about it
in their diary.

So they remember exactly what happened on this day.

Patient Name: Carl Fredricksen

Date: Sept 06

"Patient reported shaking in left hand, memory loss, and loss of balance when walking. Patient couldn't recall what he ate for breakfast. Tremor did not appear to be consistent with a diagnosis of either Parkinson disease or essential tremor. He had a CT of the brain, which was reported as normal. The patient had a complete dementia workup, including B12, TSH, BMP, RPR, monoclonal profile, and an EEG. All diagnostic studies were reported within normal ranges with the exception of both the RPR as well as Lyme titer.

Being a neurologist is like solving a mystery in someone's brain using science.

And at the end, you get to make someone feel better.

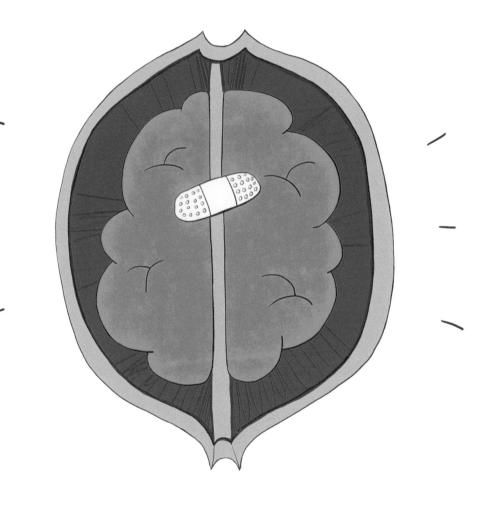

That's neurology in a nutshell.

I now pronounce you...

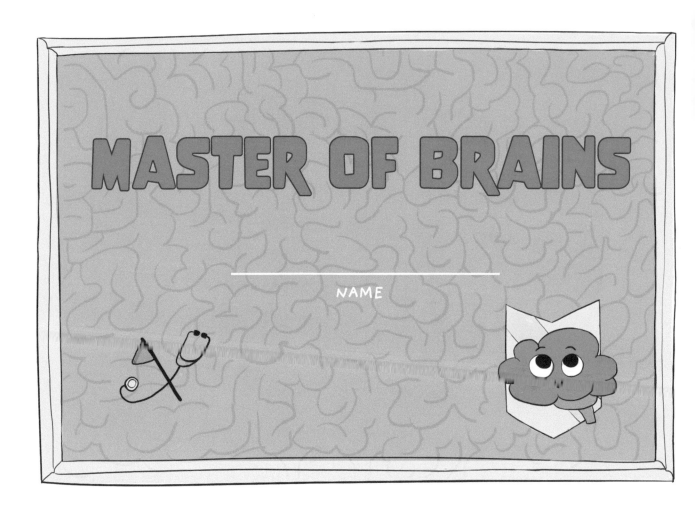

MASTER OF BRAINS

_____
NAME

ABOUT THE AUTHORS

Ali Zaman is the founder of Cabin Health, a neurology technology venture based in San Francisco. He completed his Master of Public Health from Brown University and his Bachelor's degree in neuroscience from the University of Miami. For more information, visit cabinhealth.com.

Tanya Zaman is an animator and digital artist based in Los Angeles. She has worked with leading brands and production companies like Bad Robot and Fox. She graduated with a Bachelor's degree in computer animation from Ringling College of Arts and Design. For more information, visit tanyazamanart.com or IG @tanyazamanart.

To get in touch, email us at hello@cabinhealth.com.

Dr Taimur Zaman

Ali Zaman

Tanya Zaman

New Jersey, 1997

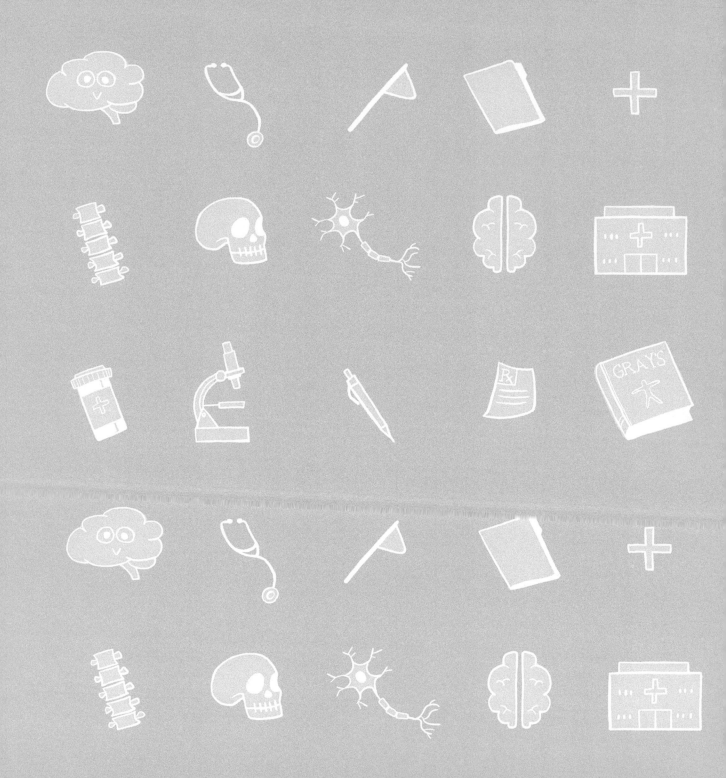

Printed in the USA
CPSIA information can be obtained
at www.ICGtesting.com
LVHW071940011123
762649LV00019B/685